Wa

Gina Mercer

Watermark

Watermark
ISBN 978 1 76109 281 7
Copyright © text Gina Mercer 2022
Cover image: Pixonaut on iStock

First published 2022 by
GINNINDERRA PRESS
PO Box 3461 Port Adelaide 5015
www.ginninderrapress.com.au

Contents

Extracts from *The Dictionary of Water*   9

Bodies of water   11
The brush of your embrace   12
In the river's lap   13
Enfolding   14
Dasyatis brevicaudata   15
Coldwater blues   17
Imperturbable   19
Tug boat   20
The device of seeing   21

Extracts from *The Dictionary of Water*   23

Cloud Bank   25
Waves of rock   26
After eight days of unremitting fog   27
Brimming   28
Finder // keeper   30
Portrait of two-year-old with tired mother   32

Extracts from *The Dictionary of Water*   33

There is water…   35
Slow-swimming koi   36
Viral acquisition   38
Irresistible tides   40

Extracts from *The Dictionary of Water*   43

Beneath the face   45
Envy its wide berth, its orbital security   47

Extracts from *The Dictionary of Water*   49

Becoming otter   51

Rapides   52

Swimming in time   54

Extracts from *The Dictionary of Water*   57

Playing opera to the Atlantic   59

Dialects of cod   62

The *Thunnus thynnus* debate   64

Extracts from *The Dictionary of Water*   67

Water the grand pianos   69

Making   71

Percussion   74

Extracts from *The Dictionary of Water*   75

Acknowledgements   76

water writes always in *(=the) plural
The 1915, Marcel Duchamp

watermark ‖ Imprint of water washed into the sheer onion-skin of every human animal.
See: *Inescapable* and *Indelible*

drink ‖ To imbibe the blessing of water. Risk of inebriation or overdose. Symptoms: 1. release 2. light-headedness 3. revelation.

swim ‖ Act of congress between bodies of water and animal. Timing of inspiration (intake of breath) crucial to successful coupling.
See: *Buoyancy* or *Bliss*.

Bodies of water

I:

Driving in from the arid airport
my eyes feast on the vastness of sky,
the mountain's grandmother presence,
this river, simple and sinuous in the sun,
arching and rippling under the wind's fingers.

This place,
this body of water, tugging
my heart back   to
this home-shaped space.

II:

Friends visit,
washes of conversation
lap and comfort.
Friends hug me home,
bountiful bodies of water
tugging my heart back   into
this home-shaped space.

The brush of your embrace

She stitches a row of bubbles across the bay
hands and feet threading through the cold clear,
leaving a trail of small silver on the river's breast.

Fish observe her shadow crossing their seagrass paddocks.

Home in the bathroom, she peels back
the black lycra, revealing –
a calligraphy of seaweed
          brushing across her breast,
a Braille of sand trailing
                    messages around her cold-sharp nipple –

In the river's lap

Long Beach, Tasmania

Thighs flinch at the Derwent's chill embrace
        urging retreat to the sand –
push in deeper,
brace for the plunge
as brain shouts   'Stop.'

Ignoring brain, and thighs,
she swims across the bay
past the ancient-mother blue gum,
past the dark araucaria standing guard by the swings,
past the grove of casuarinas emanating gentleness –

First lap is freestyle
speeded by brain-freeze,
the return is breaststroke –
that radical split screen:

air view	*underwater view*
cormorants drying	sand-bed rippling
clouds playing	fish slipping
wave chop	seagrass hair, current-brushed.

One more set of laps across the river's lap,
body numbed but getting on with it,
not impressed by the promise of stingrays.

No sightings today,
just exhilarated blood and singing muscles
the kick of escaping   gravity
the bliss of   buoyancy

Enfolding

Escaping northerly's desiccation
I head to the river – and swim –

imagine you there – beside me –
your fluid competence
kicking pain
into the calm cold
        Derwent swells holding
                your strong young limbs.

At home in this element,
        beside you in your element,
mother-daughter/daughter-mother body –
eight-limbed unison of curving strength
flowing within the river's pulse.

Today the bay holds me
                a cool, close enfolding –
but there's
        a hole in the water
                I'm missing
our liquid intimacy
            of mind   memory   name   skin.

Dasyatis brevicaudata

Swimming with you every day this summer,
I want to know your name.
It's only polite, don't you think?
This is clearly not a one-night stand.
I mean, we're sharing the same bed, river, oxygen, planet.

I learn your name: *Dasyatis brevicaudata*.
Should I call you Dasy for short, in true Aussie fashion?
No, that would be rude, we'll keep it formal. Much better.

Dasyatis brevicaudata
sounds vastly superior to short-tail
which doesn't convey your majesty at all,
not when Wikipedia tells me you are
the largest stingray species in the world.
No wonder my heart races
every time I see you.

Like anyone with a crush, I look you up,
and learn that you have:

spiracles: *black holes ridging up behind your eyes which take in
and expel water to clear sand from your gills*

denticles: *tooth-like scales on your skin*

tubercles: *hard or soft bumps on your skin*

and finally

Ampullae of Lorenzini: *a highly sensitive sensory system for detecting organisms moving beneath sand*

Really? Ampullae of Lorenzini – sounds more like saintly
relics from Firenze, don't you think?

And those spiracles
(I really thought they were your eyes)
make you look so fierce
as if you're glaring at God –

or me, for sliding my slim, kicking shadow
across your sunlit back,
across all your purposeful denticles and tubercles.

So, now I know you a little better,
Dasyatis brevicaudata
I wonder if your dark shadow shape
will still give my body
        that coffee-shot of apprehension
                each sunlit morning I swim across your bay?

Coldwater blues

November, Derwent River, Tasmania

The promise of a rare, 30°, spring day
draws soft bodies from hidey-holes.

Winter-delicate feet crinkle-scrunch
at the improbability of sand,
register pebbles as sharper than memory.
Eyes squinch at the glare
from white, winter-plump thighs.

Three women broach the river.

One plunges bravely, surfaces, yelling:
> *It's cold all right. Race you to the pontoon.*

Another begs for more time:
> *I can't feel my legs – and that's a good thing*
bobbing and dipping her way to full immersion,
finally heading out toward the bobbling, desirable pontoon.

Third woman, lingering closest to shore,
chuntering longest, declares:
*Nope, I'm not swimming out there. My head will freeze off.
It's so not Queensland.*

Turning to me, wading bystander with goggles in hand,
she repeats: *It's so not Queensland.*

As I dive beneath the iciness and lap the bay,
seeking out warm eddies,
her coldwater blues play in my head:

It's so not   Queensland.

Imperturbable

I plunge
immerse my raging
in the cold green.

Waves of anger falter
at the shock of ocean.

Immutable –
the water absorbs my hot-limbed fury
        without consequence –
all thrashing and kicking transforming into…

                an innocence of splash,
                        an effervescence of silver.

Tug boat

The black and white tug
has sole command
of the wide, wind-ribbed river.

Storybook-sturdy it steadies
through grey and white waves,
a monochrome of utility.
All the frisking sailboats of Saturday
are moored now in a sedate state of Sunday.

Tug trudges down the river
to meet an ocean-weary tanker,
gnarly rust streaking its grey flanks.
Brisk black and white tug nudges
the tanker to safe harbour, calm berth.

Tug, you are pure reassurance –
the face of my steady friend
waiting at port
after all the long, uneven voyages.

The device of seeing

kunanyi flaunts her snow –
a teenager in a new outfit.

The Derwent dimples and plays
the early evening light –
an eighteenth-century wit.

Shafts of sunset spotlight
the pink breast of a galah
on the deep green velvet grass –
a jeweller's display.

But those out walking tonight
        have eyes only for their devices.

What are snow, river, sunset, clouds, birds, the play of light –
        when you're playing Pokemon Go?

fountain ‖ Lithe performer (of clear disposition) trained by Aquarian engineers. Supplies own choreography. Incarnation of perpetual motion. Transports delight to public squares.

cloud ‖ Aerial animal composed entirely of water. Best viewed from above. Best viewed from below. Best viewed from within. Open to interpretation.
See: *Camel* or *Jellyfish*.

wave ‖ Liquid sculpture. Universal dynamic. Holds the power to: 1. rewire grieving nervous systems; 2. erode cliffs; 3. transport humans to shore and ecstasy.

Cloud Bank

I'm skipping up to the Cloud Bank. Need to fill my pockets full of clouds.
Withdraw a bundle of those shiny, light, and frothy ones – to balance out, discount,
the darkening miasmas of pandemic panic. That's the world's weather about now.

Yes, I need a stash of those small, round, flotsam clouds that frolic on high
summer skies. Frolicsome cirrocumulus. That's the currency I need.
Interest in such clouds is sky high.
Floating rates. Stratospheric.

And maybe, while I'm at it, I'll stock up on some of those spectacular, lenticular clouds.
The ones people mistake for spaceships. Maybe apply for a loan
on the futures market? Definitely wouldn't be a blue skies investment.
Happy to go into hock to get a stock of *stratocumulus lenticularis duplicatus.*
Feed my hunger for wonder.

Is there any need to worry there might be a run on the Cloud Bank in these uncertain
times? Good news is – there's never a deficit. No shortfalls. Forecasters predict
the Cloud Bank is always in surplus, can supply any level of demand.
Orographic to cirrus. Stratus to altocumulus.
Every cloud currency in plentiful supply. Your balance is always in the black
and steel-blue. Flame and cream. Purple and green. Apricot and grey.
And, of course, gold is standard, especially at sunrise.

The Cloud Bank specialises in updrafts, never overdrafts. Simply cast your eyes up.
Take in a draft. Draw down as much as you need from the endless lines of credit.
Let's skip up to the Cloud Bank.
Use our inbuilt iris scanners to open up the vaults.
Get ourselves a pocket-full, head-full, heart-full of clouds.
Feed our hunger for wonder.

Waves of rock

Rock is my muse

    I post

four monosyllables to accompany
my deep-shadowed photo –

a standing-ripple of sandstone.

water set in stone

        waves of rock

much to g(r)aze upon

          two poet friends respond.

My eyes gorge on this paradox –
    fluid rock.

Even the shrunken phone-screen image
makes me want to lie my body down,
immerse, full-length, in its steady wave –

Poets quoted (in italics) responding to my Facebook post are Dr Terry Whitebeach and Jane Williams. 12 June 2017: Burrabaroo Lookout, Prince Henry Clifftop Walk, Blue Mountains, NSW.

After eight days of unremitting fog

Varuna – the Writers House, Katoomba

I'm on retreat to write about water but –
enough already with the wet…

air, hair, ground, lungs, trees, skin
            everything is seeping and dripping,

trees too wet for roosting,
clumps of white cockatoos,
usually so raucous joyous,
slump on TV aerials,
disconsolate ducks seek
dry patches under miserable picnic tables,
even the worms are drowning.

I promise, I will still write odes and epiphanies to you, Water –

only maybe, you could let Sister Sun out to play with you,
            for just a bit?
                        Maybe, now?

Brimming

She looks normal (she hopes).
Walkers on the bush path see
        striding boots (sturdy)
        waterproof jacket (sensible)
        walking pants (comfortable)
        an ordinary woman.

After a week alone with her words
she's feeling anything but ordinary –

she's brimming

revelling in rampant bubbles
like the rain-fed creeks she fords.
Spume from all the cascading
words affects her vision.

She's in a state of joyous arousal
(no other way to put it).

Yes, she knows she should avoid
such sibilance, those semi-erotic *ou* sounds,
not to mention hyperbole and superlatives.

Yes, she knows she should avoid
the ATM and the Bamix,
she's way too trippy
to be trusted with liquidity or naked blades.

But if she could just conjure up
her lusty lover
she'd have no problem with focus,
with knowing exactly what to do
      with all this brimming.

Finder // keeper

At moonrise, we lay
a tartan rug on the cliff-top.
Lay ourselves down to drink
silver light and golden whiskey.

Our lips took turns receiving
the pewter-cool kiss
of my new hip-flask
until it echoed empty
and the moon was high and full.

In all the slidings,
kissings and moon risings,
the hip-flask lid somehow slid,
did a discreet dive off the cliff.

At low tide next day, we returned,
slightly slow with whiskey's afterglow.
You donned wetsuit, fins, and mask,
estimated height and parabola,
scientist's eyes intent,
searching the cold clear water
frilling at the cliff's base.

In spite of all the odds and whiskey
you did find that dull-grey disc –
wedged in a kelp-clad crevice.

I've kept the flask, and its lid, these forty years

and you

finder, mender, diver, lover, solver –

you are definitely a keeper.

Portrait of two-year-old with tired mother

She squats,
absorbed,
in the middle of the road.

Mother halts, ten paces ahead,
eases her many-bag burdens.

What now? We're almost home.

Sun-brown child raises her eyes,
reluctant to look away from the black road –
a splotch of engine oil
has met and mingled with the morning rain.

Rainbow fell down

Voice intent, she must
share this miracle with her mother.

Look   rainbow fell down

Her first metaphor –

rainbow fell down.

dragonfly ‖ Water's most favoured attendant. Construction: fine copper wire, iridescence of curiosity. Jeweller unknown.

fern ‖ Filed in The Archival Repository of Water under the category – DREAM.

File note (in Water's hand):
Fern is the Essence of green perfection – & somehow Myself – in the queer way of dreams

mist ‖ Soft wrap woven from the belly-fur of ringtail possums. Effective poultice for wounds of the earth and lungs. Administer in slow, deep breaths.

There is water…

when disaster phones in the middle of dinner
there is water – glass after gulping glass

when panic throttles at three a.m.
there is water – long green bath immersion

when pain straddles & thrusts
there is water – soothing waterfall in a glass cubby

when tears bloat & stain & strip
there is water – soft cloth solace

when fever escalates, hallucinates,
there is water – cool caressing temperance

when rigor mortis arrives in solemn certainty
there is water – the washing grace of farewell

when trees gnarl against dry persistence
there is water – the thrumming beneficence of rain.

Slow-swimming koi

i.m. Deb Westbury, 1954–2018

I pour soap flakes into clear water
– transformation happens –

I drop silk into milky suds
– transformation happens –
burnt-orange darkens and drowns
and then, rising from the laundry tub
                your wry-smiling face
        and this get-it-done washerwoman
becomes grief-struck friend,
eyes and cheeks awash.

Last time I saw you
I was wearing this shirt
applauding till my palms stung
as you launched your last book
beneath the old oaks of that ochre house we love.

Through runnelling tears
my shirt now looks like
                slow-swimming koi   or
autumn-leaf geometry on white-stone paths,
or, as practical Lucy, impatient with her poet-mother would say,
like what it is: burnt-orange silk soaking in a laundry tub.

My hands, those ancient agitators,
continue on, complete the task,
hang the shirt to drip dry.

Laundry water and tears soak my T-shirt,
wet patch blossoming across both nipples.
You'd laugh at that.

My soaking skin,
my tender buttons,
        feel chill
but I won't change,
not just yet,
want to steep in this memory of you
                a moment longer.

Climb the attic stairs,
email your partner,
ask for one of his poignant reports
on how you are –

computer so bloodless and click-arid
when what I want is

– the transformation that is you –

laugh flowering across the room,
glass upon glass of conversation flowing,
your saffron warmth lifting the chill from my chest –

Viral acquisition

The cure for anything is saltwater: sweat, tears, or the sea.

Isak Dinesen

She flew to Rome, my friend,
a vital conference, she said,
and there, in a font of holy water
she met a virus,

who entered   enflamed
        her brain –

now she is counting the losses

can't drive
can't meet with friends
can't work
can't play with her kids
can't ride
can't decide

exposed to freshets of laughter, ideas, conversation, music,
conflict, concepts
        (she who always relished a good concept)
too much of any of this and
                her brain   shuts down

that virus turned her world,
her brain, inside out and upside down,

38

and whenever I swim
I add saline to the sea,
weeping for my friend
who loves swimming,
year after year curing herself with immersion
in seas and lakes and pools all over the world

now even a short swim is no cure
rendering her legs so spastic
her lover has to haul her out
awkward as a beached minke

swimming for her   now
dangerous sensory overload –

light dancing through water
liquid music of bubbles
rippling rhythms of body
shifting concepts of balance and buoyancy

all make the sea no cure for her.

Irresistible tides

was it the predator's viscous spray
on your prepubescent chest?

was it the many times they pumped,
without asking, into your resisting flesh?

was it the waters that broke
bearing a rape-baby you couldn't hold?

was it your habit of drinking
the pain of others
to save them from drowning?

was it the icebergs of unwarranted guilt
bobbing, insoluble, inside?

all those
churning
insistent
tides
swamping
tugging
pushing you
towards

the ocean
bed of oblivion

all those tides
irresistible

as the siren call of the pill bottle
full of small dry shells
gleaming with white promise

the promise of
no more

bath ‖ Epiphany of solace. Long deep egg with sub-ventral blowhole. Essential qualities: 1. warm on days of pain and frost 2. cool on days of miasma and fever.

milk ‖ Water infused with emulsion of pearls and essence of summer. Best delivered via tender one-way valve in dilly of warm skin.

fruit ‖ Small highly coloured sacs invented by trees for the satisfaction of tongues. Global phenomenon. Water in high state of desirability.

burble ‖ Distinctive mating call of wild creeks. Rarely heard in cities. Species routinely driven underground, incarcerated in lightless, concrete tunnels. Such conditions have proved unconducive to reproduction or generation.

Beneath the face

for the lost Lake Pedder

We read   screed after panel-screed
of mind-numbing numbers:
cubic metres of pouring concrete
and then, the pawing water.

We learn   of drenched road-builders,
rain-slicked hands slipping on mattock handles,
benighted families
entrapped by wilderness, mud,
the isolating dreams of big engineering.

We see miles and miles of placid lake,
so seeming complete –
        serene
mirror to shimmering skies
and muscular mountain ranges
reflecting and counterpointing
in the water's face.

We sense
beneath the stillness,
the drowned
                trees and buttongrass
                spiders and orchids
                birdsong and antechinus

all decaying for decades
at the cubic pace of water

beneath
the slick surface
the deceptive reflective face
they now call

      Lake Pedder.

Envy its wide berth, its orbital security

A cruise liner has conjured itself
into the river's sunrise
and sucks on the port's teat.

Farmers and other residents resent the seasonal succubi
appearing throughout the droughty summer,
gorging on water,
draining the island dry.

Tourism operators and city fathers
see liquid gold pouring from every porthole.
They worship and murmur
the ships' names in their sleep:

Caribbean Princess   Pearl Mist   Silver Whisper
    Norwegian Dawn   Crystal Serenity…

like half-asleep men half-remembering the name
of that hyper-real sex-worker they porned last night.

Cafés bloat with the bored,
sated eyes seeking, drinking in, yet another
quaint//exotic scene in yet another dot on the itinerary.

Wander the foreign yet samely pavements,
swollen white joggers cushioning from all jolting,
all thinking about –
the clear scarce water
that swirls our shit away
makes our cocktails clink
bathes our nauseous bodies.

Traversing the mystery-deep waters
believing no trace left behind
believing in our total *orbital security.*

Italics indicate quotes from Sarah Day's poem, 'QE2', *The Ship*,
Brandl & Schlesinger, 2004, p. 67.

The island referred to here is Prince Edward Island, Canada. But water
scarcity is a global problem for cruise liners and the ports they frequent.

gutter ‖ Third-rate accommodation provided by town planners for the egress of water. Frequented by undesirable cohabitants, e.g. poisoned rats, drowned dreams, and burger wrappers.

watershed ‖ Large cavernous structure in which water stores essential mechanicals. Favoured by water as a place of sanctuary or retreat.

dam ‖ Water penned in rammed earth for the benefit of thirsty human or other animals. Achieves intense beauty despite indefinite detention. Chief advocate: The Sky.

Becoming otter

Niagara Falls, spring

grey pavement. grey road. sky – a multiplier of grey.

bouquet of umbrellas unfurl along the path: pink against
grey, red against grey, bright-white against grey. the tourists
are tired. cold. all wet grey. they are here to look. they are
saturated. they are grey tired of looking.

yet they do
saturated eyes
mesmerised by this

      fluid glass-green pouring

so much, so fast, so living,
this pouring, this torrent, pouring clear,
so clear, so swift flowing over the lip
all this curling green clarity

desire rises,
i dive in   become otter
roll over and over
      in and down the greenness

      all of me otter
            in this liquid YES lipness
      utter otter
            curving diving
                 singing defiance
                     singing NO to all the grey

Rapides

la Rivière Bow, Banff, spring

The light gets tired, he writes, & I wonder if water, too, can
get weary with all that flowing & sliding & washing away. In
the hotel swimming pool the water looks weary, constantly
banging its soft body against concrete, making the effort to
dimple up when disturbed, entered, by our alien soft bodies.
Unable to affect any kind of escape, all means of subversive
seeping or flowing thwarted by hard-faced concrete &
engineers.

But here, this river, this water, is energy is wild
filling air & eyes, slooshing the dark rock channel. No river
bed this, no slouching, idling or sleeping for this river, it's a
race, a race way, this river is spray & slalom & burble &
sing…singing clear, green, glacier, white, clarity… rushing
through & over & free – so busy & big the tourists can't talk
on their mobiles.

It's all river & strong & river & loud & over the cascade, this
miracle of light & sound & water & sound & gravity & light
& air & water & water. They might label it, confine it inside
the word [waterfall]   but this river is not falling, nothing as
passive as a fall
        not for this dynamo…

it is charging & zinging over the rocks, *rapide rapide* indeed –
it sings as it burns along, flows over, smoothing edges from
the stubborn ancient rocks, singing & zinging air & skin, all
energy & chi & off to the waiting valleys & seas & eager,
eager for its next

       transformation   incarnation…

no, this water body cannot countenance tired or weary, it is
rapide rapide along its race way

       this water, the very definition of   irrepressible.

Italics indicate quote from Bruce Beasley's poem, 'The Discredited
Hypothesis of Tired Light', *Lord Brain: Poems,* University of Georgia
Press, 2005, p. 23.

Swimming in time

I never write about time. Unlike some poets, Sarah, for instance, who writes about it with sweatless elegance, joining that long & distinguished line of poets (now, why do I see handsome moustaches at this point?) for whom Temporality is a Big Theme. But here in this overheated casket of a room (don't always trust the pictures on Airbnb), the dominating sound is the ticking of a 70s sputnik clock which I really don't love in the daytime but am trying to befriend as I sweat my way through 2 a.m. jet lag, 3a.m. anxiety, 4 a.m. hot flush & 5 a.m. intermingling of all three
& finally, I'm sweating on time, sweating through time & this clock,
it seems to me in my fever of interminable wakefulness

is taking the midnight-blue satin of time (see, there, how another time reference just crept in?), crimping that glossy oceanic fabric into fine sharp pleats. Each one is a minute, & if you listen hard enough there are even finer pleats, each one a filament of time, a second. So the clock tucks & textures the dark stifling air into a baleen whale's ventral throat grooves – fine folds that concertina & stretch
& ripple into something pretty vast & (almost) incomprehensible
that travels through the deepling dark ocean of existence
(are you more aware of Existence when you're awake in the night?
always, in the hours of light, so enfolded in the sensing & living of Now?)

& come to think of it, I wonder if whales have a concept of time? I mean, there must be some trigger (is it purely sensory?) to send them migrating, swimming from Antarctica to Hervey Bay, each year. Well, that's the deal for humpbacks but you get the idea. Don't have the time or internet right now to map all the different whale migrations that criss-cross the seasonal globe
(a new way of mapping, instead of longitude & latitude?
how might that change our way of imagining the planet, mmmm?).
Not that I wouldn't be interested in such research
but I'm trying to write about time here (first time ever)
& perhaps I should at least try to stick to that in the given time

but one more digression (or maybe it isn't?) – is it more anthropomorphic to think
that whales have a sense of time or to assume that they don't? I'm really not sure
but I am confident that dolphins know the timing of a wave to an exquisite degree,
pleating their lissom bodies through curving liquid geometry
with gymnastic precision every single time.
I mean, have you ever seen a dolphin botch a move?
Well, have you?

So, if I'm riffing on the topic of Temporality,
I should (according to the Victorian moustaches) head somewhere profound
before I finish, right? Accomplish some dolphin-smooth move
that swims you deep into philosophical waters?
Here I am wallowing about in the realm of dolphins & whales,
caught in the ripples of their existence –

& I am so very far from exquisite or elegant or even philosophical right now.
More like the sweltering dugong tumble-turning in despair in that minute,
squalid-yellow pool at the Surabaya Zoo. Dugong & I both longing
for the cool, clear embrace of rolling swells
longing to be
porpoising
swimming in our first-home
the midnight-blue sea
expanding & encompassing
as the throat grooves of time.

spray ‖ Raceme of tiny droplets to be worn on the left lapel
   of the heart on promising occasions.
   See: *Exuberance.*

humidity ‖ Infinitesimal, invisible droplets of persistence.
   Immense capacity to enervate human animals. Enemy of
   pavlovas, Blue-Tack, soft-cover books.

hooshing ‖ Song performed by water whilst falling long
   distances. Believed to soothe the anxiety of rocks.
   See: *Lullaby.*

Playing opera to the Atlantic

Ian's a social worker 40 weeks a year,
teaching mindfulness to unpredictable men.

Ian's a lobster man 12 weeks a year,
pulling 275 pots every 12-hour day.
Inheriting boat and licence
from his large, silent father
who built both boat and business.

Albert plays classical trumpet,
sails with Ian, just the two of them
out there pulling pots.
Every run is same, same:
pull one up, remove the angry spiky haul,
bait the pot, drop it back,
12 hours a day,
12 weeks a year.

But the sea
is never same, same.
It's the big boss,
unpredictable, cold –
     kill you in minutes
without rippling a muscle.

Ian respects the boss –
     dead if you don't
knowing how to swim is no protection,
wet-weather gear weights you
     down the one-way tunnel
to hypothermia // drowning.

Gotta respect the boss,
all day, every day,
one slip, one mindless moment –

you're a lump of frozen lobster-bait yourself.

Ian inherits boat,
licence and a passion
for mindfulness,
paying marine-deep attention
to every subtle mood and wrinkle
of those ice-hefting swells,
attending   every minute of every 12-hour day.

Ian's father fished
whole days without words –
mind full
        of sea.

Ian and Albert
soothe the boss
play CBC Classical,
floating opera and rolling symphonies
across vast intransigence.

Most dangerous workplace in the world.
Even if you know how to swim,
better have your mind full
        of nothing
                but the Atlantic.

This poem is based on a generous conversation with lobster fisher Ian Forgeron, Charlottestown, Prince Edward Island, Canada, October 2016. Lines in italics are direct quotes.

Dialects of cod

On Canadian radio they're playing,
not the latest hits,
but the call of the Atlantic cod, *Gadus morhua,*
and for comparison, the song of the Arcto-Norwegian cod.

The cod from North America has clearly been listening to the Blues,
his call is sexy, rhythmic, guttural – and strangely appealing.
Norwegian cod song is scratchier,
not so vibrating, not so Paul Robeson.

The radio recordings are not designed to reach out
to a potential cod demographic.
Scientists have been studying cod calls,
detecting dialect differences,
not just between Norwegian and Atlantic cod
(that, you might expect)
but it turns out that cod from Cornwall croon
a different tune to those dwelling near Aberdeen.

As the seas warm
the cod are beginning to leave their villages,
seeking waters the right warmth
for spawning and breeding.

The earnest ichthyologist from Essex
is worried that female cod in one village
won't dig the dialect of the migrating males,
won't release her eggs when he sings.

It'll get very confusing,
like when you visit Ireland
and they're speaking English but
you can't follow a word of the lilting rapid.
But for the cod, this could be really dire,
could mean there'll be fewer baby cod.

And the seas are getting noisier as well as warmer,
so the cod can't hear each other clearly.
That means even more confusion
and potential cod couples missing each other
in this overheated world.

We really must stop burning coal
and making such a racket –
for the sake of the cod and their vital dialects,
          their deep ocean blues.

The *Thunnus thynnus* debate

Bloke on his tuna-boat deck, legs planted wide and steady –

It's fuckin' crap, you know, just crap, that tuna stocks are low. There's fuckin' heaps. Come round the boat all the time, we're fuckin' handfeeding 'em. Stacks of 'em. Fuckin' guvmint's full of crap.

Wiry filmmaker making a doco about *Thunnus thynnus* airs a counter-theory –

Tame tuna? No, we reckon maybe it's starving tuna coming to the boats to get a feed. See, their main food source, the herring shoals, are small and getting smaller. Overfishing. Climate change. It all shrinks the shoals. Could be the tuna are just plain hungry.

Government scientist's clever, cautious voice enunciates –

There's no evidence tuna are starving. It might be that they're lazy, see fishing boats as an easy feeding opportunity. Tuna numbers are increasing, slowly, off a very low, endangered base. No evidence to support an increase in quota this year.

Same story both sides of the globe:
      fishers wanting more,
              activists sounding alarm,
                      scientists sounding caution.

In the interests of balance,
I'd like to interview a representative of the Atlantic blue-fin tuna community –

Please, for a few minutes, could you slow your 350-kilo sleekness for a quick chat about the current numbers situation?

Must say, I admire your camouflage – dark steel-blue on top, silver-white underbelly, designed to be invisible from above and below. So clever.

What can you tell me about your numbers right now? Decimated a few years ago, I know. Are things getting any better?

Yes, of course, I understand, it's tough for one Thunnus thynnus *to guesstimate such things when your tribe travel so far and fast.*

Gazing into your large black circle of eye, I see depth, distance, such tides of thought, circling these questions, wondering –

Why don't you lot simply leave us in peace

> *to hunt herring*
>> *to range*
>>> *wherever we please*
>>>> *in our oceans of home?*

sinkhole ‖ Subterranean act of revenge for centuries of water rights violations. Sabotage may manifest in the swallowing of: 1. cars 2. houses 3. certainty 4. whole suburbs.

mizzle ‖ A melancholic, silver spaniel. Characteristically presses against windows. Insistently seeks company.

mud ‖ A compelling coalescence of Earth and Water. Known to induce states of ecstasy in toes and other small animals.

dew ‖ A grace of water bestowed by night on the humility of grass. Converted by morning into a blessing of glistening.

Water the grand pianos

Please don't touch the pianos.
Easy rule, never played, don't plan to.
Please don't dust them.
Easy rule, I'm here to write.

Please make sure they stay warm.
Easy rule, get too hot, I'll sleep outside.
Please ensure a constant 70°F.
Easy rule, I'll not touch the thermostat.

Please be careful exiting or entering the house.
Easy rule, I'll slip in and out, lithe as a squirrel.
Please ensure no squirrels enter the house.
Easy rule, don't let the squirrels in, no matter how hard they knock.

Please don't joke, squirrels aren't cute, they're a menace.
Easy rule, no squirrel jokes.
Please consider the damage a squirrel could do to the pianos.
Easy rule, consider the considering done.

Please water the grand pianos once a week.
Easy...   what!?!
Please water the grand pianos once a week.

Please listen, see, warning lights, tubes, filtered water, special watering device.
Please repeat. I'm really jet-lagged.
Please listen: warning lights, tubes, filtered water, watering device.
Please attend, the instructions must be followed exactly.
Easy rule, don't deviate, mustn't deviate, observe the warning signs.

*

So, please tell me, how are the pianos? No, don't tell me, I'll check on them myself. *Easy now...wouldn't you like a cup of tea? I've put the kettle on to welcome you home.*

Long silence –
a flotilla of notes, lush and beautiful, floats up the stairs.

The grand pianos survived.

Making

North River, Prince Edward Island, October 2016

Clambering out of my jet-lag
I find the world outside
               is still –
sky is close
soft and grey as a galah's shoulder.

The whole suburb is mute,
lawnmowers slumber in faux barns,
late summer flowers are scentless as airport roses,
not even a small, white dog wrinkles the air.

At last, something not muted –
the odour of mudflats stomps up my nostrils,
oyster and warm mulling seaweed. Yes!
And there's my first blue jay, edges
hard to discern against a blue spruce.
Cool colours but crisp – awake!

Steel-blue heron stalks the rim of mudflat
searching, angling for its fish supper,
edges hard to discern against the silvering water.

I glance up,
catch the shimmer of another bird
against the westering sky…
        but no bird sounds like this.
A small drone. Exotic, to be sure,
but no new bird to add to my list of sightings.

Beefed-up drone operator props
against his steel-black, V8 pick-up,
legs apart, doors open, so much tech on display.
His bird-slight companion, in black and white,
hovers at his elbow
angling to gaze at the screen,
craving images of river, mudflats, sky –
          as seen by the drone.

Round the boardwalk's bend
a pregnant Japanese woman
black-clad belly arcing toward the cloud-horizon
is taking very particular photos of the river, mudflats, sky.
Abstract of greys, silvers and soft browns
worthy of Morandi –
is that what she's seeking?

Languorous, post-coital river fingers the mudflats –
          I'll flood you later – with ardour – but later – I'll do it later.

A low jumbo jet descends the grey,
we crane to observe its imminent belly.
Recent escapee from similar caverns
I think of all the febrile viruses and tragedies
fomenting within that cold metal skin.

Walking home, I see the drone operator
and his black-and-white companion,
plodding, wading on the edge of mudflat.

The drone has drowned.
Their bodies angle like angry herons
searching silvered water for lost worlds.
River ripples opaquely, nonchalant,
refusing to reveal those flooded images
       of river, mudflats, sky, river, river.

A silent clumping pilgrimage
of damp trousers and ruined shoes,
his rage palpable across the unperturbed seagrass bed,
her slender shoulders appeasing, both him and the river.

The muted sun progresses to the soft horizon
in a swirl of Turner-style cloud-light.
And there, on its right shoulder
a blur of pink, like you might see on the neck
of a turtledove if the angle is right,
a soft blush burnished by bronze.

The sun, setting, on all our attempts at making.

Percussion

Late autumn, High Park, Toronto

Dragonflies dwell by the pond
but these circular ripples
aren't made by the flying
they're made by the falling…

small early rain
dropping water onto water
making luscious dimples.

Us, caught coatless,
trusting the sun's promise,
sensible jackets left safe and dry –
                    in the car.

We saunter to shelter
as droplets dottle
our hair and shoulders –
finger-prints of rain

playing crisp percussion
on layers of yellow leaves –
a sound curiously dry and distinct,
        intriguing,
like nothing you'd ever hear at home.

caisson ‖ Large, hermetic, baseless chest in which human animals seek privacy when caressing riverbeds.

frog ‖ Pool-dwelling, freshwater selkie. Sewn from scraps of leaf-bright silk. Skin is permeable. Devoid of tail, teeth, claws, spikes, and stings. Swims at depths of vulnerability and ambiguity.
See: *Poet*.

waterhole ‖ Bird magnet. Best visited at sunset in the company of Silence.

Acknowledgements

Several of these poems were selected for publication. Thank you to the editors: Sarah Day, *Australian Book Review, States of Poetry,* 2018; Stephen J. Williams, *unfurl* 3, 2020; Vivienne Glance, 2020 *Poetry D'Amour Anthology*; and Phillip & Jillian Hall, *Burrow* 2, 2021.

The Dictionary of Water poems (which form part of this collection) are inspired by the element of Water and the Scottish poet, Thomas A. Clark. In particular, his wee book *The Pocket Glade Dictionary* (Underwhich Editions, The Coach House Press, Toronto, 1980, 16 pages). I thank him for revealing the possibilities of this poetic form – the imaginary dictionary entry. For the gift of his delightful book, I thank my talented friend Maureen Scott-Harris (Canadian poet and essayist).

In 2019, *The Dictionary of Water* poems were published in their own wee book – a limited edition of 100 copies (26 pages). It was designed by Australian Graphic Designers Hall of Fame legend Lynda Warner, and published by Wild Element Press, wild.element@iinet.net.au. Thank you to Lynda Warner and Tracey Diggins for bringing this project to fruition so brilliantly. At its launch in 2019 (Fullers Bookshop, Hobart), I performed a selection of these poems to the inspired harmonies of flute trio Silverwood. Thank you to the amazing musicians: Lynne Griffiths, Angie Bull, and Carlie Collins. It was a sheer delight to collaborate with you.

In 2016, I was selected as the Prince Edward Island Writer-in-Residence. I enjoyed a stimulating and productive month in which I wrote poems for this collection as well as connecting with many intelligent and kind people – Richard Lemm, Lee-

Ellen Pottie, Wendy Shilton, Fran Gray, Ian Forgeron, Deidre Kessler, Diane Hicks Morrow, Laurie Brinklow and all the lively participants in Richard Lemm's writing classes. Thank you to each of you and to the Tasmanian Writers Centre and the University of Prince Edward Island for running this enriching program.

Between 2014 and 2017 I served as a Peer Assessor for Varuna – The Writers House. This was an unpaid position but recompense came in the form of one week's residency per year of service. In June 2017, I enjoyed a retreat at Varuna and wrote many poems about Water. Big thank you to all who keep Varuna going (especially Eleanor Dark's family).

My generous friends keep me aloft with encouragement, insights, editing, and enlivening conversations. Thank you for your distinctive friendships: Anne Collins, Lyn Reeves, Mary Jenkins, Kristen Lang, Megan Schaffner, Liz McQuilkin, Jane Williams, Sarah Day, Irene McGuire, Robyn Rowland, Lynn Romeo, Maria Simms, Ioanna Panaretos, Em Dennes, Vick Vivian, the Heavenlies, the FFIG, and Oasis Women Poets.

I would create little without the abundant and sustaining love of my family: Bruce Mapstone, Lucy Mercer-Mapstone, Stephanie Lymburner, Shelly Hayes, Tim Bass, and Jessie Lourdesamy. Thank you isn't strong enough a word to express how much you mean and give to me. So here is a burbling cascade of clearest gratitude to each of you.

CPSIA information can be obtained
at www.ICGtesting.com
Printed in the USA
LVHW082002210322
714005LV00013B/584

9 781761 092817